INTRODUCTION

It is my hope that this small volume may prove to be of use to many who are interested in a short history, in nontechnical language, of some western plants, and of their uses by the Indians and others as food as well as medicine. To treat of all the useful and edible plants of the west would take a volume many times this size, but described here are those I consider most important or interesting, and certainly the ones most often encountered by most people.

Since some plants of the west are poisonous, it is necessary to be sure of your identification before using a plant for food, and several species must be carefully processed (such as by leaching) before they are edible. The following rules are suggested:

1. Study carefully the descriptions and pictures of the plants in this book to make sure of your identification of each species.

2. Poisonous plants are marked POISONOUS in capitals. Avoid eating these plants. The most dangerous are described on pages 54 and 57. Others less poisonous are on pages 7, 11, 27, 33, 35, 39, 41, 48, 49, 50, 52, 54, and 59.

3. If any plant has to be specially prepared before eating, follow the directions for preparation very carefully, omitting no details, and being overly careful if anything.

4. A plant with an acrid, bitter or pungent taste may be poisonous and should be left alone unless full details are given as to how to use it. Avoid all mushrooms unless you are an expert.

To aid you in identification the plants are split into easily understood divisions. Water plants, ferns and their allies are lumped together in one group, trees in another, shrubs in a third, vines in a fourth, and herbs in a fifth. At the start of the larger sections plants are also divided by color of flower.

ARROWHEAD, Tule Potato, *Sagittaria* spp.
(Water Plantain Family)

About 3' high, with flowers growing around stem in whorls of 3, and leaves sheathing stem at base. Fibrous roots and milky juice. Grows in meadows up to 6000'.

When Lewis and Clark were camped in Oregon, they practically lived on the tubers purchased from the Indians. The tubers are found several feet away from the plant. Muskrats store them in their nests, where the Indians would gather them. After boiling them, the Indians sliced and strung them up for winter use, calling them Wapato. The Chinese in California used the tubers roasted or boiled. Large tubers, 2 inches in diameter, contain a milky juice when raw that is quite unpleasant, but very sweet when roasted. In England corms are ground fine and yield a flour that can be used in making cookies, muffins or puddings. Habitat: Ponds, streams and marshes. Most states; and w. Canada.

DEDICATED TO

My husband, Nathan Sweet, whose encouragement
kept me going until the finish, and
Charles Horn, whose help and fine criticism made
this possible.

CONTENTS

Southern Goldenrod

"To win the secrets of a weed's plain heart."

James Russell Lowell

Common Edible

&
Useful Plants of The West

Muriel Sweet

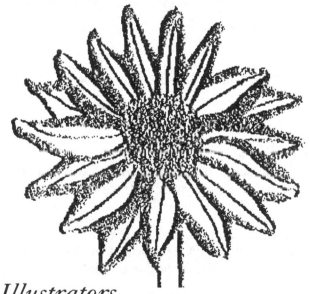

Illustrators
E. Reid, C. Yocom, B. Johnson

Naturegraph

Library of Congress Cataloging-in-Publication Data

Sweet, Muriel
    Common edible & useful plants of the West

    Includes indexes.
1. Plants, Edible--The West--Identification.
2. Plants, Useful--The West--Identification. I. Title.
QK98.5.U6S95   1976   581.6'1'0978   76-58

ISBN 13: 978-0-87961-046-3
ISBN 10: 0-87961-046-8

Thirty-third printing 2014

Naturegraph Publishers has been publishing books on natural history, Native Americans, and outdoor subjects since 1946.   Free catalog available

Naturegraph Publishers, Inc.
PO Box 1047 ● 3543 Indian Creek Rd.
Happy Camp, CA 96039
(530) 493-5353
Books for a better world   www.naturegraph.com

BRACKEN, Brake Fern, *Pteridium aquilinum*
(Fern Family)

Herb, 1'-4' high. Distinctive, dark, cord-like, rootstocks; lower pinnules of leaf toothed, upper smooth.

The root is viscid, bitterish and, like most of the fern tribe, has a salty and mucilaginous taste. When burned, the ashes yield more salt than other vegetables. Also good as fertilizer for potatoes if worked into the ground.

The astringency is so great that it is used abroad in preparing chamois leather. In Siberia and other northern countries, the inhabitants brew the roots in their ale, mixing one-third of roots with two-thirds of malt. Ancients used the roots and whole plant in decoctions and diet drinks for the spleen and other disorders. Japanese use it in soup. Indians boiled and ate the root stocks, as they are starchy; also used them as a diuretic and worm medicine. In early days the tops were used in the spring, while still curled, as asparagus. Pioneers would soak them in water with wood ashes for 24 hours, then cook the young leaves like pot herbs. The fern was also used in a decoction as a cure for rickets in children. Bracken has been found to be poisonous to livestock if eaten extensively. Habitat: Ponds, streams, etc.; open woods; meadows; streamside woodland. Most states, and w. Canada.

CATTAIL, *Typha* **spp.**
(Cattail Family)

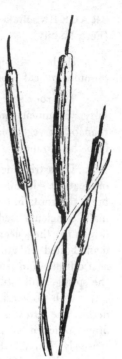

Rush-like plant 3'-7' tall, with very long, slender leaves and typical sausage-shaped catkins, forming feathery tips with age.

The Greek, Dioscorides wrote: "the starchy substance mixed with axungia (hog or goose grease) is good to heal burnings, it doth moderately cleanse and dry, and being applied to bleeding places stancheth blood."

Our Indians made much use of the leaves for chairs and mats. In winter leading shoots of root stock are filled with starchy material and are used as a salad or cooked as a vegetable. Root stocks are also dried and ground into meal, being equal in food value to rice or corn. The people of Bombay, India, harvest the pollen and make bread from it. Young flowering shoots, before pollen has developed, are eaten either raw or boiled and considered a great delicacy.

Root stocks are more valuable than seed as food for wild life. Geese and muskrats eat the starchy underground stems. The plants form nesting shelters for many marsh birds. Habitat: Ponds, streams, etc.; marshlands. Most states; and w. Canada.

HORSETAIL, Scouring Rush, *Equisetum arvense*
(Horsetail Family)

Eaten by Romans in 7th century, the young heads were boiled like asparagus, or mixed with flour and fried. Indians and early settlers used the stems as a stimulating diuretic in kidney and dropsical disorders.

The outer layer of the stem contains a quantity of silica useful in polishing hardwood, ivory and brass; also used by Mexicans and Indians for scouring pots. Aconitic acid in plant is poisonous to horses but not to cows or goats. Bears and musk rats eat it, and rootstocks are eaten by geese. Habitat: Oak woodland; streamside woodland; coastal coniferous forest; montane coniferous forest. Most states; and w. Canada.

INDIAŃ POND LILY, Yellow Water Lily, *Nuphar polysepalum*
(Water-lily Family)

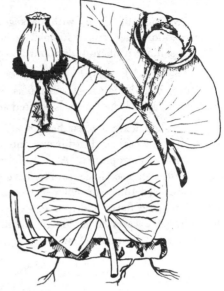

Large leaves rise from thick rootstock. Rootstocks baked; seeds for bread and soups. Habitat: Lakes and ponds. Most states, and w. Canada.

WATERCRESS, *Nasturtium officinale*
(Mustard Family)

The prostrate or ascending stems grow from wet places or in water; small white flowers in racemes. Naturalized from Europe.

Xenophon recommended it to the Persians to make children strong and it was much prized by the Moslems. Romans considered it excellent food for people with deranged minds.

Parkinson in 1640 says, "Leaves or juice applied to the face or other parts troubled with freckles, pimples, spots or the like, at night and washed away in the morning. The juice mixed with vinegar to the forehead is good for lethargy or drowsy feeling."

Coronado found it near the Gila River in Arizona and in 1769 Padre Crespi speaks of it. In 1806 Lewis and Clark found it in Oregon. Indians used the plant for liver and kidney trouble and to dissolve gallstones. It is now commonly used for salads and to garnish other dishes. Habitat: Ponds, streams, and marshes. Most states; and w. Canada.

CALIFORNIA BAY TREE, Oregon Myrtle, California Laurel, *Umbellularia californica*   (Laurel Family)

Tree 50'-100' high, with dark green leaves that have a strong, pungent odor when crushed; small greenish-yellow flowers in clusters of 6-10; solitary fruits turn dark purple. In shaded areas.

The wood is yellow-brown, takes a high polish, and is used for furniture, boat building, etc. Indians wore a leaf under their hats to treat a headache. The fruit was roasted and eaten.

Crushed leaves, when held near the nose, will produce severe headache or sneezing. Both leaves and seeds contain an oil reputed to have anesthetic properties. Also useful in nervous disorders, intestinal colic, and as an insecticide (said to drive away fleas and lice). The small limbs are used today on chicken roosts as a louse preventative. The leaves are good flavor additives to stews, roasts, etc. Hung up with garlic to dry, they prevent molding. Habitat: Streamside woodlands; oak woodlands. California and sw. Oregon.

CALIFORNIA BUCKEYE, *Aesculus californica*
(Buckeye Family)

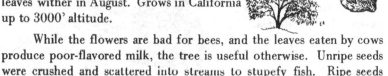

Tree 12'-25' high, with 5 finger-like, light green leaflets to each leaf; beautiful white flowers in candle-stick-like spikes, turning into round, brown balls in the fruit; leaves wither in August. Grows in California up to 3000' altitude.

While the flowers are bad for bees, and the leaves eaten by cows produce poor-flavored milk, the tree is useful otherwise. Unripe seeds were crushed and scattered into streams to stupefy fish. Ripe seeds contain a bitter, poisonous principle.

Leaves were steeped to make a tea as a remedy for congestion of the lungs and varicose veins. Seeds were buried in swampy, cold ground during the winter to free them of the toxic bitter quality, and eaten in the spring, boiled. The wood was used for making the fire drill. Habitat: Foothill woodland.

CALIFORNIA FAN PALM, *Washingtonia filifera*
(Palm Family)

These palms grow in moist alkaline soil below 3500' and are 20'-75' tall, with leaves 3'-6' long, torn almost to the middle, making a ragged appearance. The fruiting spadixes hang 8' to 21', bearing large clusters of berries that sway in the wind.

Berries turn black when ripe and are eagerly eaten by birds and animals. Orioles use the threads from the leaves for nests.

The Indians would roast and eat the berries; also grind them into flour for cakes. Strings from the leaves were used in basket weaving. They would sometimes cut the terminal bud to roast and eat as a great delicacy, but this would cause the tree to die. Leaves were used to thatch their houses and the trunks were sometimes used as building timber. Habitat: Desert scrub; streamside woodland. California.

CALIFORNIA WALNUT, *Juglans californica*
(Walnut Family)

Tree 15'-35' high, or
shrub; dark bark;   9-17
leaflets.

The brown nuts are
edible. Habitat: Oak
woodland. S. California.

JOSHUA TREE, *Yucca brevifolia*
(Lily Family)

A long-armed, scraggly tree, 16'-30' high, usually growing in high
deserts of around 3000'-4500' altitude. The dark brown bark is marked
off into small square plates; narrow sharp leaves 6"-9" long; greenish-
white flowers in thick panicle, 8"-14" long.

The Indians made a red dye from the red rootlets, which were also used for weaving patterns in baskets. The flower buds were eaten hot
or cold after roasting. They were sweet because of high sugar content
and were often given as candy to the children. The pioneers used the
wood for fence posts. Habitat: High desert. SW states.

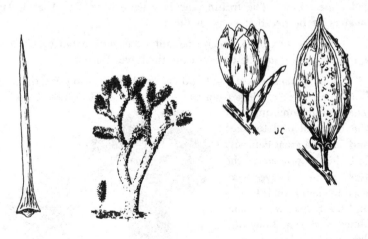

OAKS, *Quercus* spp.
(Beech Family)

The oaks form a large genus of about 200 species. Acorns of the Black Oak (*Q. kelloggii*), and the Blue Oak (*Q. douglasii*) seem to be the favorites, though several others were used by the Indians. However, they were careful to keep different kinds of acorns separate.

The acorns were soaked overnight to make it easier to get the kernels from the outer shell. After they were shelled and dried, the meats were ground into a flour or meal. If possible, the meal was put in a sand hollow, and covered with twigs of Douglas Fir, Cedar or White Fir to break the force of the water poured over to leach the meal (a sieve could be used in place of sand). This was done about ten times. To remove the meal, the hand was pressed on it and the adhering meal put in a basket. Any sand that was in the meal was washed out by pouring water through the basket. Hot stones were used in cooking meal. Often meal was leached through cedar twigs for flavor.

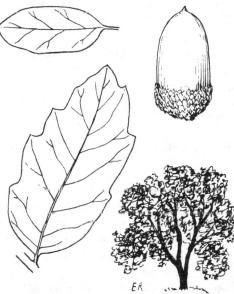

Soup, bread and a pudding were made from the meal or flour. One kind of bread was made by wrapping the dough in fern leaves and baking in hot ashes. Leavened bread was made from the Water Oak (*Quercus nigra*) of eastern Texas and many southeastern states. A small amount of ashes was added to the dough, which made the bread rise. It was baked in an earth oven.

Sometimes acorn meal was allowed to accumulate a mold. The mold was scraped off, kept in a damp place, and used to heal boils, sores and other inflamations. Habitat: Oak woodland; streamside woodland. Oregon, California, Arizona.

PINES, *Pinus* spp. (Pine Family). Noted for their slender needles in bunches and large cones; all produce edible pine nuts in the cones, but the following species are especially sought:

DIGGER PINE, *P. Sabiniana*
(Pine Family)

Has three needles in bunch; a branching tree growing in the lower altitudes of most mountains of California away from the coast. The soft center of the green cone, roasted for about 20 minutes in hot ashes, yields a sort of syrupy food that was much relished by the Indians. Seeds are rich in fat and proteins and are usually eaten raw. Yellow pitch from the tree is a protective counterirritant. Bark infusion reputed useful for consumption. Twigs and leaves used in decoction for rheumatism. Twigs and rootlets used as sewing material for baskets. Charcoal from nut meats crushed and applied to sores and burns. Habitat: Foothill woodland. California.

TWO-LEAVED PINYON PINE, One-leaved Pinyon Pine, *P. edulis* and *P. monophylla*

Both are desert mountain trees with short needles and small cones. Seeds are rich in protein and used as food by Indians. The nuts were pounded and made into cakes or cooked as a gruel. Cones were picked before they fell and put on a fire to loosen the nuts or seeds. Often a soup was made from the nuts to give to babies.

Habitat: Pinyon-juniper woodland. Utah, Nevada, California, Arizona.

SUGAR PINE, *Pinus Lambertiana*

Very tall tree, with thick foliage; needles in bunches of 5; large, long cones; sweetish sap.

The sap yields a saccharine that is very sweet, but acts as a cathartic if very much is eaten. Powdered resin was used by the Indians for sores and ulcers. The hardened sap was dissolved and used to wash sore eyes; pitch was used to mend canoes, to fasten arrowheads and feathers. Nuts and shells were pulverized until like butter, then eaten or put into soup. Habitat: Montane coniferous forest. Oregon, California.

WESTERN YELLOW PINE, *P. ponderosa*

Tall pine with 3 long needles in a bunch, bark on older trees yellowish and picture-puzzle-like, smelling of vanilla. The gummy pitch from the bark is very adhesive and was used by the Indians for canoes and on huts. The mistletoe that grows on this pine was used in a decoction as a stomach aid and to relieve colic. Habitat: Montane coniferous forest. Most states, and w. Canada.

LODGEPOLE PINE, *P. contorta*

Usually has a straight trunk, but scraggly branches; needles in 2's and 1½"-2¾" long. The buds where chewed by the Indians for sore throat, and pitch was put on open sores. The inner bark was mashed into a pulp and made into cakes. These cakes were put between skunk cabbage leaves, a fire of wet material was made on top of them, and they were left to bake for an hour or more. Then they were smoked and put away after being pressed into firmness, to be used on trips. Habitat: Coastal coniferous forest; montane coniferous forest. Most states; and w. Canada.

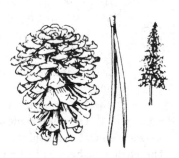

WESTERN WHITE PINE, *P. monticola*
(Pine Family)

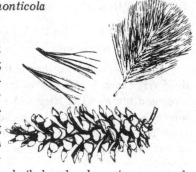

Also called Silver Pine. Bark whitish or reddish and smooth; needles in 5's and very slender, 2"-4" long; cones 6"-10" long, are very slender when closed, and green or dark purple when young. The young shoots were boiled by the Indians and used for rheumatism, kidney trouble, boils and coughs. Bark was boiled and a decoction was made for stomach disorders. The pitch was used to fasten feathers to arrow shafts; it was also rubbed on the shafts to make them stronger and more elastic.

The young, inner bark of most pines could be used for food, in cases of starvation, by thorough pounding. Habitat: High montane forest. W. states, and w. Canada.

WHITE ALDER, *Alnus rhombifolia*
(Birch Family)

Also other species of *Alnus*. A tree 15'-30' high, with light green leaves, whitish to gray bark, green hanging catkins, and small, brown, cones ½" long.

Parkinson, in 1640, writes of *Alnus*: "Leaves and bark are cooling and drying. Fresh leaves laid on tumors will dissolve them; also stays inflammation. Leaves with morning dew on them, laid on a floor troubled with fleas, will gather the fleas and can then be quickly thrown out. A black dye was made from the bark."

Indians used a decoction of dried bark to induce circulation, check diarrhea, allay stomach-ache, facilitate childbirth, check hemorrhages, and, mixed with Indian tobacco, to induce vomiting. They also made a dye that was yellow-brown. Early settlers made charcoal and used it in the preparation of inferior gunpowder. The astringent bark and woody cones were used for tanning leather. For dye, the bark was peeled in the spring. Habitat: Along streams. W. states, and w. Canada.

BARBERRY, Oregon Grape, *Berberis* spp.
(Barberry Family)

An erect-growing shrub, with holly-like
leaves, fragrant yellow flowers in racemes,
followed by bluish berries, and growing from
sea level to 5000' altitude; most are bushes,
but *B. repens* (Creeping Barberry) crawls low
over ground. All are lovely garden shrubs
with bronze-crimson, autumn leaves. The
wood is of a beautiful yellow color, used by
Spanish-Americans to make neck crosses
(crucifixes).

Juice of the fruit fermented with sugar
makes an excellent wine; also a jelly made
from the juice is very tart but very good served with meat. Berries boiled
in soup add flavor. Indians used roots and bark for ulcers, sores and as a
tonic, also in a decoction for consumption, heartburn and rheumatism.
Bark and roots are made into a yellow dye. Leaves are chewed for acne.
Liquid from chewed root was placed on injuries and on wounds, while
cuts and bruises were washed with a root decoction. Root tea was used
for blood tonic, cough medicine, and kidneys. Habitat: Wooded slopes.
W. states, and w. Canada.

BEAR CLOVER, Mountain Misery, *Chamaebatia foliolosa*
(Rose Family)

Indian name is Kitkitisu. It is called "Mountain Misery" because
of the properties of the leaves that cover all clothing with sticky black gum.

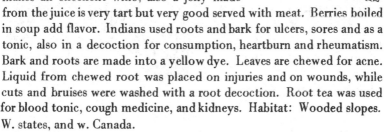

The plant is a low-growing shrub not over
2' high, with small, white, strawberry-like flowers; fruit brown; leaves finely dissected and fern-
like.

Indians used plant for many ailments:
leaves were steeped in hot water to make tea used
for rheumatism, skin eruptions, etc.; leaves also
used in a decoction for coughs and colds. Sometimes used as a medicine to treat venereal diseases.

Flowers and fruit fair forage for deer and
stock. Plant fine for erosion purposes due to the
mat of roots and closeness of growth, but resinous leaves unfortunately make it a fire hazard.
Montane coniferous forest. California.

BLUE CURLS, Vinegar-weed, Camphor Weed, *Trichostema* spp. (Mint Family)

Woolly Blue Curls, *T. lanatum* (pictured) is a shrub, but most other species of this genus are herbs. The shrub is 2'-4' tall, but the herbs range from 3"-16". The shrub has blue or purple flowers (rarely white) and more or less hairy leaves. The name of Vinegar Weed comes from the penetrating and acrid odor of the foliage of all species.

Indians made a decoction of leaves and flowers for colds, ague and general debility; a bath of this decoction was taken against small-pox; leaves were chewed and put in cavity of aching tooth; fresh leaves were mashed and thrown in streams to stupefy fish. A major honey plant. Most habitats. Calif. to B.C.

BLUE ELDERBERRY, *Sambucus mexicana, S. caerulea* (Honeysuckle Family)

These species are very closely alike, but *mexicana* usually has 3-5 leaflets in a compound leaf, while *caerulea* has 5-9 leaflets. Both species are bushes or small trees, 6'-15' high, with small white flowers in terminal clusters turning into bluish berries.

The Indians call it "the tree of music", as they make flutes from branches that were cut in the spring and then dried with the leaves on. When thoroughly dry, they would bore holes in the branches with a hot stick. The long shoots were used for arrow shafts. Berries were used in several ways, for a drink and also dried and stored for winter. Flowers were used fresh, externally in a decoction for an antiseptic wash for skin diseases, and taken internally to check bleeding of the lungs. The inner bark yields a strong emetic. Habitat: Open places. Calif. to w. Canada.

CASCARA SAGRADA, *Rhamnus purshiana*
(Buckthorn Family)

An attractive shrub, 4'-6' high in south; up to 30' in the north, where it is a fine bee plant.

Early Spanish settlers learned from the Indians of its wonderful medicinal qualities, and called it Cascara Sagrada, or "sacred bark." Indians would girdle the tree at two points three feet apart and make vertical cuts between, then peel off the bark and dry it for medicinal use as a laxative. For best results bark should be gathered in autumn or

early spring. A small piece of bark put in cold water for 12 hours is used for a tonic. Habitat: Montane coniferous forest; coastal coniferous forest; streamside woodland. Wash.; Id.; Ore.; Mont.; Calif.; w. Canada.

CEANOTHUS, Wild Lilac, Sweet Bush, Buck Brush, Deer Brush, Blue Blossom, *Ceanothus* spp.   (Buckthorn Family)

The species shown is Common Buck Brush, *C. cuneatus*. Bush or small tree, 2'-20' high, with rigid, sometimes spine-like, branchlets; leaves with tiny stipules at the base; blossoms white through blue to lavender, borne on plumy spikes and usually giving off a spicy odor; commonest on open slopes where there is good drainage. It gives fine protection from erosion and is good in gardens.

The Indians used the seed as food and the blossoms as a fine lather when rubbed briskly on the skin. The leaves are suitable for use as a tobacco; bark and roots are used as an astringent and tonic. The red roots also yield a red dye.

The plant has medicinal properties serviceable today. One variety is beneficial as a blood coagulant, also for coughing and tonsilitis, and as a stimulant tonic for mucous membranes. It overcomes mal-assimilation of food, and influences beneficially acute inflammation of the liver and spleen. Habitat: Open places and woodlands. W. states, and w. Canada.

CHAMISE, *Adenostoma fasciculatum*
(Rose Family)

A spreading shrub, 2'-10' high, with slender, wand-like branches and graceful, pyramidal clusters of white flowers in June; fruits gray; new bark is reddish, turning gray when old. It is quick to catch fire due to resin in leaves. If burned, the first year's leaves are grazed by stock and deer. Bees frequent the blossoms for pollen; goldfinches and woodrats eat the seeds.

Indians used an infusion of bark and leaves to treat syphilis; also an oil yielded by the plant was used for skin infections. Sick cows find benefit from the plant by chewing on the leaves.

The wood burns very quickly with a bright flame and supplies quick heat for cooking. Habitat: Chaparral or brush. California.

CHOKECHERRY, *Prunus demissa*
(Rose Family)

Shrub 3'-8' high, with 3-10 white flowers in short clusters; berries bright red or purple. Extensive thickets.

Inner bark used by Indians as a tonic to check diarrhea and to relieve nervousness. A decoction of young shoots and bark was taken. There were several ways to use the berries. Acid was leached out of fresh berries with water through basket, then they were ground in a stone mortar; the dried pulp was boiled and eaten. Fresh

berries were also ground and dried for later use. Berries make a good jelly or jam, and wine is sometimes made of them.

There is hydrocyanic acid in the young leaves, which is dangerous for cattle, but it is lost by fall. Animals and birds eat fruit. Habitat: Chaparral or brush; montane woodland. Most states.

CHRISTMAS BERRY, Toyon, *Heteromeles arbutifolia*
(Rose Family)

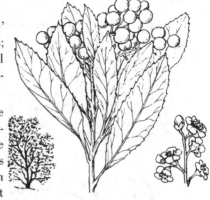

An evergreen shrub, 6'-10' high; with simple, serrated leaves; flowers white, in small terminal clusters. Grows in the foothills below 4000' altitude.

Early-day Californians made a drink from the berries, and fishermen in the Channel Islands used the bark to tan their fish nets. Indians boiled the berries and baked them in their ground ovens with hot stones for 2 or 3 days. They also stored berries for a few months, then parched them and made them into meal. Habitat: Oak woodland; chaparral or brush. California.

CREOSOTE BUSH, *Larrea divaricata*
(Caltrop Family)

An erect-growing and many-branched bush from 2'-9' tall; leaves appear divergently 2-lobed; yellow flowers solitary and terminal; foliage very resinous and strong-smelling. The roots put out an inhibitor to keep other plants from growing too near. But, in seasons of heavy or frequent rains the inhibitor is washed from the ground and then you will see flowers and small plants growing around these bushes. As the soil dries, the inhibitor starts again and the neighbors leave in a short time.

Creosote yields a coloring matter, and a gum (lac) secreted by a scale insect, which the Indians used to attach arrow tips to the shafts of fire-hardened wood.

Creosote was considered to be a cure-all by many Indians. A decoction of the leaves was used for stomach disorders, chicken pox, kidney trouble, colds, snake bites, rheumatism, venereal diseases, sores, and tetanus. Powdered dry leaves used for sores. Strong tea used for tonic and mixed with badger oil as a burn ointment. The Spaniards used a preparation for sick cattle and saddle gall on horses. Habitat: Desert scrub. SW states.

EMORY'S INDIGO BUSH, *Dalea emoryi*
(Pea Family)

Shrub densely and diffusely branched, 1'-4' high; leaves in clusters of 5-7 leaflets; small branchlets spiny; pealike, lavender flowers in short spikes.

Indians crushed the flowers of the various species of *Dalea* and steeped them in water to release a yellow dye used in art work. A dye was also extracted from the glandular twigs. The roots of *Dalea terminalis* have a sweet taste and were eaten like candy by the Hopi. Flowers were also used medicinally and for food.

A tea made by boiling the stems was used as a remedy for many ailments including: colds, coughs, pneumonia, tuberculosis, stomach ache, smallpox, kidney trouble, venereal disease, measles, muscle pains, and diarrhea.

Stems were chewed for toothache; crushed stems used for sores. Habitat: Desert scrub. Calif.; Ariz.; Nev.

EPHEDRA, Joint Fir, Mormon Tea, *Ephedra californica*
(Ephedra Family)

Shrub, 1'-2' high, and with long, jointed stems; opposite and scale-like leaves; slender stalks often broom-like and green.

Ancient medicinal plant, used by the father of Chinese Medicine, Shen Mung, in 2698 B.C. Dried roots and stems, used in treatment of coughs, for colds, headache and fever. Stems sold in Chinese stores under name Ma-Huang. Chinese species is what the alkaloid ephedrin is made from; our species has a high percentage of tannin.

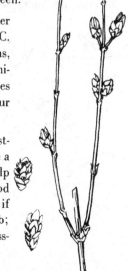

It was a beverage for Indians as well as roasted and ground for bitter bread. One tribe made a decoction of the entire plant and drank it to help stop bleeding. Pioneers made a tea used as a blood purifier. Deer and sheep eat bark and foliage, if food is scarce. Quail eat seed. Habitat: Desert scrub; pinyon-juniper woodland; chaparral or brush; grassland. California.

FREMONTIA, Flannel Bush, *Fremontia californica*
(Sterculia Family)

A scraggly-growing shrub 6'-
15' high on slopes from 1500' to
5500' altitude. Leaves have a brown
soft fuzz underneath; flowers are a
lovely yellow, borne all along the
branches, making an extremely beautiful sight in early spring; the four
to five-celled capsule has grayish-
brown seeds. Local people call it
"Slippery Elm", as the inner bark
is quite mucilaginous when wet.

The inner bark is used as a demulcent for poultices (a soothing
agent for raw membranes). Cattle will browse the twigs, which are
very nutritious. Habitat: Pinyon-juniper woodland; montane coniferous
forest; coastal coniferous forest; chaparral or brush. California.

GOAT NUT, Jojoba, *Simmondsia chinensis*
(Box Family)

Bush, 3'-10' high, with gray-green leaves; the
rather nondescript petalless, greenish flowers form
head-like clusters, each female flower turning into
a smooth, brown, cylindrical capsule like an acorn.
Forms a very good stock feed on heavily grazed
land.

Indians used seeds by roasting and grinding
them for a beverage; oil of the seed was used as a
hair tonic. Fruit has a nutty flavor and early Californians made a beverage that was used as a coffee
substitute, by roasting and grinding nuts, mixing
them with yolks of hard-boiled eggs, then boiling
with milk and sugar. Habitat: Desert scrub; chaparral or brush. California, Arizona.

MANZANITA, *Arctostaphylos* spp.
(Heath Family)

The two most common species are the Green Leaf (*A. patula*, illus.), and the Grey Leaf (*A. mewukka*) or Indian Manzanita. Neither of these will fire-kill, but sends out new shoots from the large, round root crowns. A few other species do. All are evergreen shrubs, to twelve feet, with very crooked branches; attractive, small, urn-shaped, pink or white flowers are in small, nodding terminal clusters. The berries are round and of many colors, but are chiefly various shades of red and pink.

Indians made many uses of the berries, eating them raw, cooked or ground into meal to be used as a porridge. They ranked next to acorns in food value. A cider was made from the berries, which were crushed, and then scalded with enough water to equal the bulk of the berries. When settled, this made a fine drink. A jelly is also made from the Grey Leaf Manzanita and some other species.

In a medicinal way, fruits and leaves were crushed for their astringent properties for relief of bronchitis, dropsy and other diseases. A tea made of the berries was used as a wash for poison oak. The leaves were crushed and dried and mixed with tobacco to make up a smoke. Manzanita is poor forage for cattle, but many animals eat it. Habitat: Coastal coniferous forest; montane coniferous forest; chaparral or brush; oak woodland. Wash.; Ore.; Calif.; Nev.; Utah; Ariz.

MESQUITE, *Prosopis* spp.
(Pea Family)

Large shrub or small tree, 10'-35' high, with fern-like leaves and yellow flowers in slender spikes. Will grow below 3000' in mountains. Habitat: Desert scrub. SW states.

Indians mixed gum from the bark with mud to kill lice; a blue stain is made to paint the face; fruit or pods are pounded with seeds and eaten or mixed with water for a sweet drink. Pods and seeds made into meal are eaten by horses. The honey is of good quality. Deer eat foliage and twigs, while other mammals and birds eat the seeds, bark and leaves. Gum sometimes found on bark is soaked in water and the liquid used as an eyewash.

MOUNTAIN MAHOGANY, *Cercocarpus* spp.
(Rose Family)

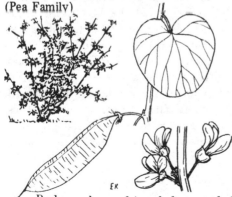

An evergreen, drought-resistant shrub or low tree; young shoots are reddish-brown, covered with a hairy down; flowers greenish, often turning brownish, whitish or reddish; fruit with a long, feathery, twisted tail giving the bush a silvery look in the sunshine. Rich, dark brown, mahogany-like wood is hard and tough, but also brittle, making a hot fire.

Indians used wood for fish spears, arrow shafts, and pointed sticks for digging. Inner bark made a purple dye. Bark used in a tea to treat colds; also they peeled the bark, scraped the inner layer, then dried and boiled it for lung trouble. The powdered young plant, stirred in water, was used as a laxative. Spanish-Americans hung branch on bed to discourage bedbugs. Habitat: Chaparral; oak woodland. Most states.

PACIFIC BLACKBERRY, *Rubus vitifolius, R. ursinus*
(Rose Family)

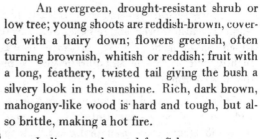

Stems 1'-8' long, erect as a bush, or trailing over the ground. It is covered with straight, sharp thorns; leaves with double-toothed edges; flower white; edible berries black. Habitat: in or near woods. California to British Columbia.

REDBUD, Judas Tree, *Cercis* spp.
(Pea Family)

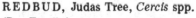

Clustered stems 8'-15' high; leaves round, heart-shaped at base; red-purple flowers appear before leaves.

Indians use bark of the young shoots for baskets; medicinally they form a mild astringent in treating diarrhea and dysentery.

Buds can be used in salads or made into pickles. The wood takes a very fine polish. Habitat: Chaparral; oak woodland. SW states.

SCARLET SUMAC, *Rhus glabra*
(Sumac Family)

A large shrub or small tree, with fern-like leaves, greenish flowers and bunches of red fruit which contain malic acid. The dried ripe fruit is slightly sour, astringent and diuretic (increasing the flow of urine).

Indians crushed the fruit to make a drink, and also dried berries for winter use. The split bark and stems were used in basket making. They gathered leaves after turning red for smoking, and roots for a yellow dye. A poultice was made of bruised leaves and fruit and applied to the skin for skin diseases. Habitat: Streamside woodland. Most states, and w. Canada.

SERVICE BERRY, June Berry, *Amelanchier* spp.
(Rose Family)

Shrub 3'-12' high, sometimes a small tree 15'-20' high, growing on dry slopes in mountains or along nw. coast. Flowers white, fruit purplish-black to brown.

Europeans made pies and puddings from the berries, always leaving in seeds as they added to the flavor. Indians dried the berries for winter use, also crushed them to make a cake from which they would break off a piece to add to soup or vegetables. They made a sort of pemmican of pounded berries and dried meat with animal fat to be carried on long trips. An eye wash was made from boiled green, inner bark. Habitat: Montane coniferous forest; streamside woodland. Most states, and w. Canada.

SHADSCALE SALTBUSH, *Atriplex canescens*
(Goosefoot Family)

A roundish, gray bush, 1'-5' high, with flowers in narrow spike-like panicles, gray to dull green; the leaves covered with tiny white hairs and bran-like scales; fruit bracts are toothed as shown, on the wings (in illus.). Bushes often cover vast areas, or are associated with creosote bush and sagebrush, generally in moderately saline dry soil.

Indians ground seed for meal and also used them as an emetic. Leaves sometimes eaten as spinach. Zuni Indians in New Mexico ground roots and blossoms moistened with saliva to use for ant bites. Also stirred ashes of Saltbush into batter of their water bread in order to change color of meal to greenish-blue. White New Mexicans chew green leaves with a pinch of salt to relieve bad stomach pains. Absorbs selenium (poisonous) from soil if it be present.

Shadscale has high forage value due to the nutritive quality and evergreen habit, also richness of the seeds in sodium and other salts. Deer eat twigs and foliage; ground squirrels, rabbits and kangaroo rats eat seeds and leaves. Habitat: Desert scrub; chaparral, pinyon-pine. Calif., Ariz., Nev., and New Mexico.

SNOWBERRY, Waxberry, Indian Currant, *Symphoricarpos* spp.
(Honeysuckle Family)

Erect shrubs of low or medium height, with slender branches, sometimes prostrate and sometimes spreading by suckers; leaves opposite, round or oval; white or rosy flowers appear in terminal or axillary clusters; round, waxy-white berries.

Saponin, a poisonous drug, is contained in the leaves only. Indians made a decoction for colds and stomach-ache by pounding and steeping the roots. The fruits act as an emetic and cathartic (strong laxative). As a honey plant, it is fairly important, producing a white honey. Most habitats. Most states, and w. Canada.

SQUAW BUSH, Skunk Bush, *Rhus trilobata*
(Sumac Family)

Bush, 2'-7' high, of rocky foothills. Pale yellow flowers appear before leaves; berries red and hairy.

Parkinson (1640) writes that both Pliny and Dioscorides say of the genus: "A decoction of leaves or seed made with vinegar and a little honey is quite good against gangrene or cankers. Juice taken out of leaves by boiling them in water and, after they are strained, boil them again with some honey. Helps the roughness of tongue and throat. Decoction of green leaves makes the hair black. Plant is much used in wardrobes, chests, etc. to keep out moths—."

Brooks Botany says its astringent properties made it useful in tanning leather. Indians powdered berries, making a lotion used in treatment of smallpox. Dry powder was put on open sores, but when pustules were unopen, the lotion was put on. The fruit is eaten and a stem decoction is good for coughs. Peeled and split stems used for twined baskets. Lemonade Berry, *Rhus integrifolia*, has red berries used in making drink. Sugar Sumac, *Rhus ovata*, has a sweetish, waxen substance covering the red berries, which was used by the Indians to make sugar. Habitat: Chaparral or brush; oak woodland. Most states.

THIMBLE BERRY, *Rubus parviflorus*
(Rose Family)

A spreading bush, 3'-6' high; bark becoming shreddy with age; leaves 3"-7" wide,
usually with hairy and glandular stems; white
or pinkish flowers; the soft, light-red berry is
sweet and edible. Habitat: Oak woodland; coast-
al coniferous forest; montane coniferous forest. Calif., Oreg., Wash.,
Idaho, and w. Canada.

WILD ROSE, *Rosa californica*
(Rose Family)

A scraggly bush, 3'-6' high. Grows along stream and river banks;
pretty, light pink flowers, bright red hips (fruit). Father Font of the
Anza Expedition speaks of gathering and eating them right from the
bush. Rich in Vitamins A and C.

Indians made a tea from the tender root shoots for colds; seeds
were cooked for muscular pains; leaves and hips steeped and drunk
for pains and colics. The old straight wood was used for arrow shafts.
Spanish-Californians made jelly from the ripe fruit and ate hips raw
from the bush, after the first frost softened the hips. The leaves and
petals were astringent and used in perfume. Petals, peppermint, lemon
peels and linden leaves made into a tea for arthritis or dyspepsia; petals
also said to help dissolve gallstones.

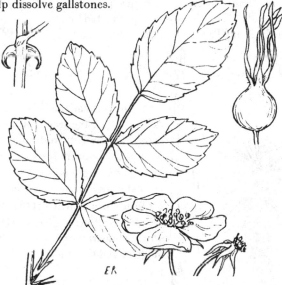

YERBA SANTA, *Eriodictyon californicum*
(Phacelia Family)

Shrub 2'-8' tall, with leaves distinctly woolly on the undersides and with strongly netted veins, the upper surface shining; flowers of terminal panicles shade from dark lavender through pale lavender to white.

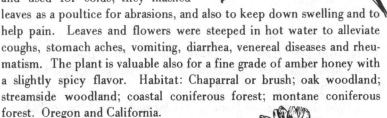

Indians boiled leaves for tea and used for colds; they mashed leaves as a poultice for abrasions, and also to keep down swelling and to help pain. Leaves and flowers were steeped in hot water to alleviate coughs, stomach aches, vomiting, diarrhea, venereal diseases and rheumatism. The plant is valuable also for a fine grade of amber honey with a slightly spicy flavor. Habitat: Chaparral or brush; oak woodland; streamside woodland; coastal coniferous forest; montane coniferous forest. Oregon and California.

YUCCAS, Amoles, *Yucca* spp.
(Lily Family)

Shrub, 2'-18' high with thickly clustered, sharply pointed leaves; large, whitish flowers form towering, terminal panicles; black seeds. The flowers are pollinated by the night flying Pronuba moth.

Indians eat the flowers. The stalks are rich in sugar; the leaves produce a fiber used in making baskets and mats. The roots are used as a substitute for soap and for cleaning hair. The large, pulpy fruits of *Y. baccata* are eaten raw, roasted, or cooked and dried for future use. Cattle eat the flowers. Leaves are pale yellowish green. Habitat: Desert scrub; chaparral or brush. Calif., Ariz., New Mexico, and Colorado.

COMMON GOURD, *Cucurbita foetidissima*
(Gourd Family)

A creeping vine, with coarse, hairy leaves, fairly large, yellow flowers and green-striped fruit balls. Called Calabazilla by Spanish Californians and Chili Coyote by Mexicans.

Indians crushed roots and pith of fruit for soap to wash clothes, but were careful to rinse several times due to prickly hairs. The seeds, ground, were eaten and portions of the gourd made a strong purge, though an overdose can prove fatal. They made a tea for bloat in horses and also for worms. The top of the plant was supposed to cure ailments of the head, and roots of the feet.

Indians along the Rio Grande would grind roots and mix with water as a laxative. Navajos used dried gourds as rattles in their dances. Pharmacopia says, "pulp of green fruit mixed with soap applied to ulcers and sores; leaves used medicinally." Habitat: Oak woodland; grassland; sagebrush; desert scrub. Most states.

WILD CUCUMBER, *Marah* spp.
(Gourd Family)

Also called Manroot and Big Root Chilicote. A trailing or climbing vine, with ivy-like, thin leaves; flowers small, greenish-white; large, green, prickly seed pods. When pods are ripe, they pop open and scatter large brown seeds covered with a soapy pulp.

The Indians roasted the seeds and ate them for kidney trouble. Decoction of plant was drunk to treat venereal diseases; oil extracted from seeds was used for falling hair; crushed roots mixed with sugar were applied to saddle-sores of horses; the crushed pieces of green roots were put in streams to stupefy fish. Juice of root is very bitter. Mexicans used for tanning. Habitat: Streamside woodland; oak woodland. Wash., Oreg., Calif., and w. Canada.

WESTERN VIRGIN'S BOWER, *Clematis ligusticifolia*
(Buttercup Family)

Climbs by aid of the petioles of the opposite and compound leaves; flowers with white, petal-like sepals, but no petals; leaflets 5-7; flowers turn into feather-like seeds. Called Yerba de Chivato, "herb of the goat" by Spanish-Americans who used it to wash wounds.

Indians used white portion of bark for fever, leaves and bark for shampoo and a decoction of the leaves was used on horses for sores and cuts. From fibers they made snares and carrying nets. Pharmacopia says it is useful in treatment of skin diseases, ulcers, colds and many eruptions. In 16th century, doctors used it internally in powdered form to treat bone pains. Habitat: Streamside woodland; oak woodland; coastal coniferous forest; montane coniferous forest. Most states, and w. Canada.

WILD GRAPE, *Vitis californica*
(Grape Family)

Vine 5'-60' long with clusters of small, greenish or white flowers.

Grapes are edible and good thirst quenchers. Used for jellies, preserves, and drinks. Habitat: Streamside woodland; oak woodland. Oregon and California.

ALUM-ROOT, *Heuchera micrantha*
(Saxifrage Family)

Perennial, 1'-2½' tall with stout rootstock (having alum-like taste); basal leaves round and toothed; long flowering stems have panicles of small white flowers.

Indians eat leaves first in the Spring, boiled and steamed. After steaming, some are dried and stored for future use. The pounded root, wet, was used on sores and swellings; steeped, it was used as an eye-wash; also small amounts drunk to stop diarrhea. A tonic of the boiled roots was taken a half-cupful a day for general debility, or three half cups a day to stop fever. The drug, Heuchera, is antiseptic and astringent. In Materia Medica, alum-root is given for gastroenteritis, nausea, vomiting, etc. Habitat: Montane coniferous forest; coastal coniferous forest; streamside woodland. Oregon, Washington, California, Idaho and w. Canada.

ARROW-LEAVED BALSAMROOT, *Balsamorhiza sagittata*
(Sunflower Family)

Herb, 8"-26" high, with tuft of large basal leaves, naked stems, few yellow flower heads, and thick root. Contains a volatile oil with turpentine-like odor; reported to be POISONOUS.

Important forage plant. Indians winnowed and cracked the seeds as food. The root was peeled, boiled and ground; then cooled and drunk for rheumatism or headache. A small cupful was taken for rheumatism and patient covered, as the drug caused profuse perspiration. The mashed root or the dry, powdered root was applied as a dressing for syphilitic sores; also mashed root used for swellings or insect bites. The gummy root sap was swallowed for consumption. Most habitats. Most states, and w. Canada.

BITTERROOT, *Lewisia rediviva*
(Purslane Family)

This perennial herb is almost stemless, with a rosette of oblong fleshy leaves growing at the top of a carrot-shaped root. The large rose or white flowers have 8-15 petals. Related species have similar qualities.

Indians would gather the root in the spring when the outer coating, which contains most of the bitterness, will slip off easily when put in boiling water. The root is quite starchy, but very nutritious and was an important food among the Indians. In fact, so much importance was given to it that a sackful of the roots was considered a good exchange for a horse. The roots were often boiled with other wild foods in a soup. Pounded dry root was chewed for sore throat. Habitat: Sagebrush scrub; chaparral or brush; oak woodland; montane coniferous forest; coastal coniferous forest. Most states, and w. Canada.

BOISDUVALIA, *Boisduvalia* spp.
(Evening Primrose Family)

Herbs, usually 1'-5' tall, with leafy stems; flowers small, white or purple, in axils of leaves or in leafy spikes; 4 petals, each 2-lobed. In low, damp ground.

Seeds yield an oil and were also used by Indians as food: Shaken into basket and parched. Habitat: Streamside woodland; meadows; coastal coniferous forest; montane coniferous forest; grassland; oak woodland. Wash., Idaho, Oreg., Calif., Nev., and w. Canada.

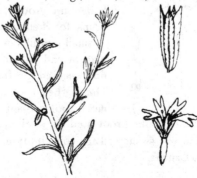

BOLANDER'S YAMPAH, *Perideridia bolanderi*
(Carrot Family)

Herb, 1'-2' high, with small
white or pinkish flowers in thick
umbels; leaves opposite, the leaflets
thread-like.

Indians gather roots in large
quantities and eat them raw or cooked as a staple article of diet—equal
to Mariposa Lily bulbs. When eaten
cooked, roots were boiled until
mealy, peeled, and cooked as soup;
this usually being done at the end
of the acorn season. If stored, they were preserved by drying and washing. Found in drier parts of west, 3000'-8000' altitude. Habitat: Sagebrush scrub; meadows; subalpine forest. Oregon, California, Idaho,
Wyoming, Utah, and Nevada.

BUTTERCUPS, *Ranunculus* spp.
(Crowfoot Family)

(*R. californicus* illustrated). Usually showy yellow (sometimes
white or red) flowers, 8"-24" high, rising from more or less basal leaves.

Young flowers are preserved in vinegar as small pickles. The juice
of flowers makes a yellow dye. Indians parched seeds and made meal

to use in bread. Roots were boiled
and eaten. One species, *Ranunculus sceleratus*, Cursed Buttercup,
has a poison, aenonal, that causes
intestinal inflamation. If the acrid,
burning juice is tasted, spit it out.
Habitat: Meadows. Most states.

CALIFORNIA FUCHSIA, *Zauschneria californica*
(Evening Primrose Family)

Much branched herb, 1'-3' high with rather fragile, green to gray-hairy leaves, and large fuchsia-like flowers. Found on dry benches and rocky hillsides.

Leaves reported used as a detergent in washing, and a dusting powder for cuts, wounds and sores on horses. Indians drank a decoction of leaves for tuberculosis, kidney and bladder trouble, and for a cathartic; also made into a poultice for running sores. Habitat: Grassland; oak woodland; sagebrush scrub. California.

CHIA, *Salvia columbariae*
(Mint Family)

Plant grows mostly below 4000' in open, dry areas. It is 3"-15" high, with 2-3 whorls of small, blue flower heads on stem.

Indians gathered seeds by bending the stalks over a basket and shaking the seeds into it. Seeds are similar to flax seed and were parched and ground to be cooked later as gruel. Medicinally, it was used to sooth inflamed digestive organs; also a bit of seed-paste put in the eye

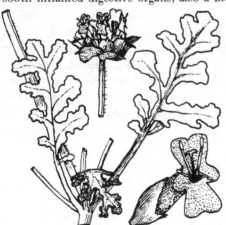

at night gathered all particles of dirt by morning due to the mucilaginous quality of the wet seed. Seed-paste is also used for soothing inflamed membranes and as a poultice for gunshot wounds. Spanish Californians made a fine drink by mixing a teaspoonful of ground seed in a glass of cold water for a few minutes, often adding sugar and lemon juice. Habitat: Sagebrush scrub; chaparral or brush; oak woodland; grassland. California, Utah, Arizona, and Nevada.

CLARKIA, *Clarkia* spp.
(Evening Primrose Family)

(*C. elegans*, Elegant Clarkia, illustrated on left; *C. pulchella*, Beautiful Clarkia, on right). Herbs, 1'-3' high with lance-like or ovate leaves; showy, purple or rose-colored flowers in terminal, nodding racemes; petals greatly constricted at base.

Indians collected seeds, which they dried, parched and pulverized, then ate the meal dry or with acorn meal. Habitat: Grassland; oak woodland; chaparral or brush; sagebrush scrub. Most states, and w. Canada.

COAST TARWEED, *Madia sativa*
(Sunflower Family)

Aromatic, glandular herb, 1½'-3' tall, with large, yellow or white flower heads; stout stem rigidly branched.

Oil is expressed from the seed and the cake used for cattle feed. It is a good table oil and a lubricant. The oily content of the seed is very nutritious and the Indians would gather them in summer and grind into a fine meal to be eaten dry. They also scalded the seeds, yielding an oil used in soap making. For their medicine, flowering tops were a poison-oak remedy and a tonic of the leaves was reported useful in treatment of inflammatory rheumatism. Northern California Indians made a cough syrup by drying the buds. Habitat: Grassland; cultivated or otherwise disturbed areas. Washington, Oregon, California, and w. Canada.

COLUMBINE, *Aquilegia* spp.
(Crowfoot Family)

(*A. formosa*, Crimson Columbine, illustrated). Most species grow in moist situations along streams or in meadows. They vary in height from a few inches to 5'. Flowers are red or yellow, five-petaled, with long hollow spurs extending backward.

Parkinson writes in 1640, "Leaves commonly used in lotions for sore mouths and throats. A dram of seeds taken in wine with saffron opens obstructions of liver, and good for jaundice, causing profuse sweating." Spaniards used to eat a piece of the root in the morning on fast days. The Indians often boiled and ate the leaves in the spring. The boiled roots were used in a tea to stop diarrhea. The ripe seeds were mashed, moistened and then vigorously rubbed in the hair to discourage head lice. Fresh roots were mashed and rubbed on aching joints. When roots and leaves are boiled together it makes a decoction that can be taken in one-half-cupful doses several times daily for a couple of days to stop biliousness or dizziness. If the whole plant is boiled it is supposed, as a decoction taken in small doses, to stop venereal diseases. Habitat: Coastal coniferous forest; montane coniferous forest; chaparral or brush; oak woodland; subalpine forest; alpine fell fields. Most states, and w. Canada.

COMMON CAMAS, *Camassia quamash*
(Lily Family)

Five species occur in the west. About 2' tall, with single, tall flower stalk coming from middle; flowers mostly a brilliant blue, but sometimes almost white. Grows in moist ground and wet meadows.

Bulbs are very nutritious and are highly thought of by Indians who will travel a long way to gather them. After the seeds are ripe in the spring, they dig up the bulbs with long, crooked sticks (usually made of mt. mahogany). Then a fairly deep hole is made and lined with fire-heated stones. Bulbs are placed inside and covered with hot ashes and stones and allowed to cook for 24 hours. They are eaten right from the fire or the black outer coating is peeled off and the bulb pressed by hand into a flat cake and hung to dry in sacks, becoming a tid-bit at feasts.

A molasses was also made of bulbs by boiling in water until it was almost evaporated. The early California settlers learned the value of the bulbs and would make pies of them. But eaten to excess, the bulb will act as a purgative and emetic. The greenish white flowers of the Death Camas often grow with the blue and care must be used in digging bulbs. Habitat: Meadows; montane coniferous forest; coastal coniferous forest; Most states.

COMMON SUNFLOWER, *Helianthus annuus*
(Sunflower Family)

The coarse, many-branched, rough stems grow 3'-6' tall; leaves about 6" long; large yellow flower heads.

Roasted seeds are good to eat. Spanish used the seeds to make a meal or gruel. Indians capitalized upon the seed oil to grease their hair, boiling the flower heads to get it. Roots were used in combination with other roots for snake bite, and a root decoction was used as a warm wash for rheumatism. A purple and black dye was extracted from seeds for clothes and baskets; also a yellow dye was derived from the plant. Roasted seeds or shells crushed and sifted were used as a drink like coffee. Ripe seeds parched and made into a meal or bread are very nutritious. Stalks yield a fiber.

Pharmacopia says, "Seed diuretic, yields a blond fixing oil; the plant is anti-malarial." Bees make a fine, amber honey from the flowers. Sunflower oil is fed to sheep, cattle and poultry; claimed to be better than linseed oil. Most habitats. Most states, and w. Canada.

COMMON THOROUGHWORT, Boneset, *Eupatorium* spp.
(Sunflower Family)

Herbs, 1'-4' tall, with hairy branches at top; flowers in nodding groups of heads or flat-topped clusters, white, pink or red; no ray flowers; leaves mainly opposite, especially in white-flowered species.

Flowering tops gathered in full bloom and stripped from stalk, are dried and kept to make into bitter tonic or tea. Tonic is cathartic and emetic (causing vomiting). The tea is taken cold as a tonic; a hot infusion is used for malarial fever. Indians called it Ague Plant due to its malarial healing quality. Habitat: Streamside woodland; oak woodland; montane coniferous forest; coastal coniferous forest; cultivated or otherwise disturbed areas; pinyon-juniper woodland. Wash., Idaho, Oreg., Calif., Nev., Utah, New Mexico, and Ariz.

COMMON YARROW, Milfoil, *Achillea millefolium*
(Sunflower Family)

A fairly showy plant, 1'-3' high, on long stems with finely divided leaves and flat-topped, white flower clusters (rarely yellow); foliage appears grayish from numerous tiny hairs.

Leaves reported to stop bleeding of wounds and to heal inflamation. Powdered, dry herb, taken with Plantain water, will halt internal bleeding and juice put in the eye will take away redness (says Achilles). Oil made from the plant stops falling hair.

The Indians picked and dried the whole plant. They put a handful of the dried material in a small amount of boiling water and used as a tonic for rundown conditions and indigestion. The leaves were used as a poultice for rash. Most habitats. Most states; w. Canada.

COW PARSNIP, *Heracleum lanatum*
(Carrot Family)

Herb, 3'-10' high; stout and coarse, with large leaves (up to 12" across), divided into three parts, hairy underneath, sawtooth edged; white flowers in umbrella-shaped compound umbels.

Tender leaves and flower stalks are sweet, used by Indians for green food before flowers appear. The lower part of the plant was a salt substitute. Indians also cooked the roots like rutabaga. Early Spaniards made a medicine compounded from the roots for rheumatism. Pharmacopia says root and leaves acrid, irritant, POISONOUS: reputed carminative (useful in expelling gas); stimulant for dyspepsia (indigestion). Indians inserted root pieces in tooth cavities to stop pain. For sore throat, they mashed root, soaked in water and used infusion as a gargle, or applied it as a poultice around the throat. Habitat: Streamside woodland; coastal coniferous forest; montane coniferous forest. Most states, w. Canada. NOTE: Resembles Hemlock.

CUDWEED, Everlasting Flower, *Gnaphalium* **spp.**
(Sunflower Family)

(*G. palustre*, Lowland Cudweed, illustrated). Herbs, 4"-36" tall, with aromatic scent and usually woolly leaves. Small, white, yellow, purplish or reddish flowers, in numerous rounded pearly heads at tops of stems with woolly, papery feeling. It is poor forage.

Indians used leaves for catarrhal infections, and decoction of the leaves for intestinal and pulmonary catarrh (inflamation of membranes); also for bruises. The bruised plant assists in healing wounds, and an infusion (steeping leaves in cold water) is used for increasing perspiration. Habitat: Streamside woodland; oak woodland; coastal coniferous forest; montane coniferous forest; chaparral or brush. Most states.

CURLY DOCK, *Rumex crispus*
(Buckwheat Family)

Herb 1'-4' high, with dark green foliage; the leaves have very wavy margins and are crisp. It is a naturalized weed from Europe.

Ancient Arabs used the roots for purging and some took a decoction with beer or ale to purge the liver and cleanse the blood. A decoction of roots in vinegar was a most effective remedy for scales and running sores. Dioscorides said the root eaten took away the pain of stings by scorpions.

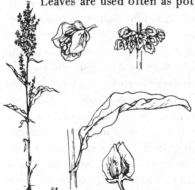

Leaves are used often as pot herbs and as an antidote to scurvy; also as a mild astringent and, in small doses, as a tonic. Indians cut roots and steeped in boiling water for a tonic and a stomach remedy; also, they washed roots and applied them to sores and swellings. Most habitats. Most states, and w. Canada.

CYMOPTERUS, *Cymopterus* spp.
(Carrot Family)

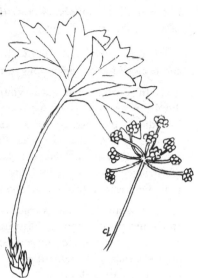

Small herbs with more or less finely divided leaves; the yellow, white or purple flowers generally in ball-shaped umbels, often appearing perfectly round and congested; the wings or ribs of the seeds have undulate margins.

Basal leaves, white flowers and parsnip-like roots were eagerly sought after by Indians. They prepared them by drying and stored for later use. Only in young state can tubers be eaten. They were usually boiled.

Water from old roots boiled was used as an insecticide. Most habitats. Most states.

FALSE HELLEBORE, *Veratrum californicum*
(Lily Family)

Plant 3'-7' tall (sometimes called Corn-Lily), with large heavily ribbed leaves which gradually grow smaller as they reach the top of the plant. Flowers are a dull greenish white, borne in a showy, elongated terminal cluster. Roots are few and extremely black.

The plant inhabits moist meadows and along streams at middle altitudes in mountains. Blossoms are said to be poisonous to many insects. Powdered roots are used as an insecticide. The dry root, powdered, was used as a snuff.

The Shoshones and other Indians used the raw root, crushed and mashed, to apply to snake-bite wounds on man and animals. A decoction of the root was taken as a tea for venereal disease. The raw root, chewed, aided sore throats, inflamed tonsils and colds. Habitat: Marshlands; meadows; montane coniferous forest; coastal coniferous forest. Most states, w. Can.

FIREWEED, *Epilobium angustifolium*
(Evening Primrose Family)

Herb 1½'-8' tall; willow-shaped, reddish leaves; lilac-purple, rose and even white flowers in long, terminal racemes.

In Europe and Asia, young shoots were used like asparagus. Canadians use young leaves and stems as a pot herb. It is used as a tea adulterant in England. Plant is astringent, and used in domestic remedies for an intestinal astringent.

It is an important range feed and honey plant. Habitat: Cultivated or otherwise disturbed areas; meadows; streamside woodland; coniferous forest. Most states.

GOLDENROD, *Solidago* spp.
(Sunflower Family)

Herbs, 1'-7' high, with usually simple stems rising from a woody base or underground stem. The small, yellow flower heads are in panicles, racemes and cymes. *S. californica*, the California Goldenrod, is very common in California fields (illustrated). Stems usually densely leafy.

Indians boiled leaves and used decoction to wash on wounds and ulcers, then sprinkled powdered leaves on wounds. The same remedy was used for saddle sores on horses. A yellow dye was made. Spanish

Americans used the fresh plant mixed with soap for a plaster to bind on sore throats. Pharmacopia says it is astringent, diaphoretic (increasing perspiration), and used for cleansing sores.

The Missouri Goldenrod, *S. missouriensis* (of Br. Columbia, Oregon and east , told by its unusually long-stemmed and fluted leaves) had the leaves eaten as a salad. Habitat: Meadows; grasslands; oak woodland; coastal and montane coniferous forest. Most states, and w. Canada.

GRINDELIA, Gum Plant, Resin Weed, *Grindelia* spp.
(Sunflower Family)

Herbs usually 1'-6' high, rather resinous, especially around the flowers; single to branched stems; rather stiff pointed leaves with toothed edges; large yellow flowers solitary, or few in a cluster.

Brooks Botany says: "Root in spring dried and powdered, makes a fine medicine for purging or hemorrhages. The decoction of the whole plant is famous for wounds and, in England, it was used for ulcers." Spanish Americans boiled buds and flowers until water was down to a pint, then that was drunk for kidney trouble. For rheumatism, fresh plant was crushed and applied to body part. Official use of drug: fluid extract made from flowering top and leaves, a stomach tonic, anti-spasmodic; also, fluid extract painted on surfaces affords relief to those suffering from ivy or oak poisoning. Absorbs selenium (poisonous) from soil if it be present.

Indians boiled root and drank tea for the liver; buds on the plant were dried for use with smallpox; a decoction of leaves was made for running sores; flowering tops, collected in the spring, were used for a blood purifier and to relieve throat and lung trouble; a small quantity of decoction held in the mouth, but never swallowed, helped to cure toothache. Small doses of a decoction of the plant were taken each day for smallpox, also a half cupful a day for measles. A half cupful hot was said to be good for pneumonia. Habitat: Marshlands; sagebrush scrub; cultivated or otherwise disturbed areas; grassland. Most states.

HEDGE MUSTARD, Western Tansy Mustard, *Descurainia pinnata* (Mustard Family)

Erect plant, 2' tall; leaves once or twice divided into small segments, ashy color. Small, yellow flowers appear on long slender stems. Found in dry areas.

The Mexican name is Pamito and is sold in their drug stores. The seeds are crushed and used as poultices or made into a tea for summer complaint. Leaves, picked young, are good boiled.

Indians gathered seeds by knocking them into baskets. The seeds were stirred over an open fire in a pan, then ground and made into a mush or stirred into soup. Pomo Indians mixed the seeds with their acorn meal for better taste. In Mexico the seeds were made into a poultice for wounds. Brooks wrote: "It is said to be an attenuate, expectorant and diuretic, and is strongly recommended in chronic coughs and hoarseness." Habitat: Desert scrub; grassland; oak woodland; sagebrush scrub; chaparral or brush. Most states.

HIGH MALLOW, *Malva sylvestris* (Mallow Family)

Erect or branching herb, 1'-3½' high, with rounded, heart-shaped leaves; small flowers are pink-veined against purple, appearing clustered or single. Grows in waste places and in cultivated fields.

Pliny wrote, "that anyone taking a spoonful of mallows will be free of disease; they soften and heal ulcers and sores." Parkinson wrote: "Leaves and roots boiled in wine or water or in both with parsley doth help to open the body, for hot agues. Leaves bruised and laid on the eyes with a little honey take away the inflammation from them."

Chinese eat the leaves raw in salad or boiled as spinach. Spanish-Americans use the plants by boiling leaves and making a wash for any bodily disease; headaches are cured by adding salt and vinegar to mashed leaves. Indians use leaves, soft stems and flowers, steeped and made into a poultice for running sores, boils and swellings. An infusion of dried leaves is good for coughs. Habitat: Grassland; sagebrush scrub; cultivated areas. Most states; w. Canada.

HORSETAIL, *Equisetum* spp.
(Horsetail Family)

See page 8, for description.

HOUND'S TONGUE, *Cynoglossum grande*
(Borage Family)

A medium-sized plant, 1'-3' tall; leaves mostly basal; blue to lavender flowers are funnelform on terminal panicles. Its leaves have a disagreeable taste and the burs stick to stock.

Dioscorides says (in regard to the genus): "the leaves boiled in wine and salt applied to bruises, or juice boiled in hog lard cures falling hair; same is good for burns. Distilled water of herb and roots good for all purposes, inwardly to drink for ulcers and outwardly heals wounds."

Roots were cooked by the Indians and eaten to relieve colic. A poultice was made of the roots for scalds and burns. Habitat: Oak woodland; coastal coniferous forest; montane coniferous forest.

INDIAN SOAP ROOT, Amole, *Chlorogalum* spp.
(Lily Family)

Herb 2'-3' tall, with narrow, fluted leaves, a brown, fibrous-coated bulb, and white petals with green veins.

Indians dug up the large bulb and stripped off the outer fibrous mesh, which was left to dry. These dried fibers became a fine brush, being tightly tied together with more fibers at one end for the handle. The inner mucilaginous layer was scraped and worked into the handle, then put in the sun for a day or two to harden. Most habitats: Grassland; oak woodland. Most states, and w. Canada.

INDIAN TOBACCO, *Nicotiana* spp.
(Nightshade Family)

(*N. bigelovii*, Indian Tobacco,
illustrated). Herbs 1'-5' tall (except
one shrub with yellow flowers, *N.
glauca*), with strong-scented, nar-
cotic-poisonous leaves, and large
white or greenish-white flowers.

In early days the leaves were
used for ailments of the chest and
lungs by making a syrup in distilled
water. A tobacco leaf was applied
to the head to relieve pains and
migrain. Seeds eased pains of toothache and leaves were burned for
ashes and used as a toothpowder. Distilled juice put in cuts, sores and
old wounds, promoted healing. Indians gathered the whole plant when
seeds were ripe but leaves still green. They dried and crumbled the
leaves for smoking. A mixture of different leaves was used with the
tobacco, such as bear-berry and sumac, also the scraped bark of dog-
wood. Indian women smoked tobacco only to cure colds. A decoction
of powdered leaves was drunk as an effective emetic (to cause vomiting).
The plant is reported to be POISONOUS to stock. Habitat: Cultivated
or otherwise disturbed areas; streamside woodland; oak woodland. Most
states.

LAMB'S QUARTERS, Goosefoot, Sowbane, *Chenopodium* spp.
(Goosefoot Family)

(*C. murale*, Nettle-leaved Goosefoot, illustrated.) Usually many-
branched plants, 1'-4' tall, with small green flowers on spiked panicles;
often strongly scented. Many species are introduced weeds.

Indians boiled the leaves as
spinach, sometimes eating them raw.
They would gather the seeds and
grind them into a meal to be stored
for future uses, such as bread making.
One variety was boiled and applied
as a poultice to reduce swellings;
also, used in the mouth to relieve
toothache. For rheumatism, the affected parts were washed with a decoction of the leaves. Most habitats.
Most states; and w. Canada.

LOBED GODETIA, *Godetia biloba*
(Evening Primrose Family)

Herb, 8"-30" tall, with narrow, alternate leaves; flowers showy, red, purple or cream colored, in racemes or spikes; petals often with purple dots near base.

Indians gathered seed pods early in the spring and hung them up in bundles to dry. When thoroughly dry, the seeds were beaten to loosen their shells, then winnowed, parched, pulverized, and stored for eating during the winter. The Indians also made a decoction for an eye wash. Habitat: Oak woodland; grassland. Oregon, California.

LOBELIA, *Lobelia* spp.
(Bellflower Family)

(*L. cardinalis*, Scarlet Lobelia or Cardinal Flower, illustrated.) Herbs, 1'-2' high, with leafy-bracted, red, yellow, white or blue flowers, which are two-lipped and highly irregular; leaves alternate.

Indians used the root and plant of Red Lobelia for syphilis and for expelling or destroying intestinal worms. An overdose acts as a narcotic. Milky juice of the plant is POISONOUS. It is a diaphoretic (increasing perspiration). Materia Medica suggests using the Blue Lobelia for prostration following influenza, and the Red Lobelia to help sticking pains in the chest on taking a long breath. The Shoshones made a tea of Lobelia for use as an emetic (to cause vomiting) and a physic. Habitat: Streamside woodland; ponds, streams, etc. Most states; and w. Canada.

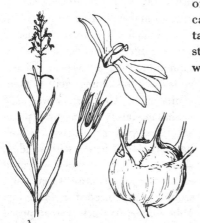

LOCO WEED, *Astragalus* spp.
(Pea Family)

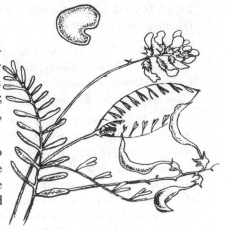

(*A. bicristatus,* Crested Rattle-weed, illustrated.) Usually bushy herbs with long stalks; alternate leaves with several to many leaflets; flowers in spikes, racemes or heads, purple, pale yellow or white.

Indians chewed the plant to cure sore throats and to reduce swellings. The boiled root was made into a decoction to wash granulated eyelids and for toothaches.

The plant grows only on soils containing selenium, a cumulative poison. It is POISONOUS to practically all stock, although, after they have once tasted it, it is much sought after by them. It is said that if poisoned stock are fed hot lard and moved immediately to new pasture, they may survive. Most habitats. Most states.

MILKWEED, *Asclepias* spp.
(Milkweed Family)

(*A. mexicana,* Narrow-leaved Milkweed, illustrated.) Usually tall, slender plants, 2'-5' high; leaves 2"-6" long; flowers usually with turned-back sepals and of various colors; stems show milky juice.

POISONOUS to livestock. Indians dried and removed sheath from stalk after cutting. On outside of woody center was a fiber covering. This was removed and made into string, also fish nets. Milk was collected and rolled until firm enough to make chewing gum. Green plant was collected when very small and boiled in two waters to use as greens. Pods and stems were eaten; roots boiled and eaten with meat. Sometimes the plant was boiled and added as a thickening agent to manzanita cider. One variety was used for inflammatory rheumatism (probably *Asclepias cryptoceras*, which has very broad leaves with sudden, sharp points). The juice was used as a healing application to cuts and wounds; also used for tattooing. Milk applied to warts was supposed to entirely cure them. Most habitats. Most states, and w. Canada.

MINER'S LETTUCE, *Montia perfoliata*
(Purslane Family)

A dainty-looking plant with 6"-12" stems, and narrow, basal leaves. Halfway up the stems, disks or cups completely encircle the stem. Above this, on a continuation of the stem, are clusters of pink or white flowers.

Fleshy, tender leaves are eaten green or cooked by the Indians, who also made a tea of the plant and used it as a laxative. The miners used the leaves as salad greens, hence the name. Habitat: Montane coniferous forest; coastal coniferous forest; oak woodland; chaparral or brush. Most states.

MONKEY FLOWERS, *Mimulus* spp.
(Figwort Family)

(*M. guttatus,* Common Monkey Flower, illustrated.) Generally herbs with opposite leaves; the flower two-lipped and yellow, purple, red or violet, with the throat open or closed by a palate (obstruction); usually plants are 1'-2' tall.

Indians used both young stems and leaves for salad greens. Root of Yellow Mimulus used as astringent. Raw leaves and stems were applied when crushed to rope burns and wounds as a poultice. Most habitats. Most states, and w. Canada.

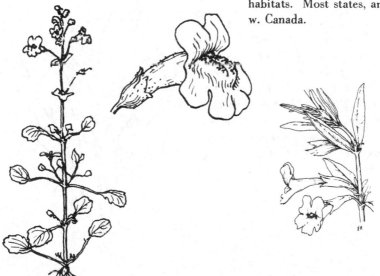

MULE EARS, *Wyethia* spp.
(Sunflower Family)

Most *Wyethia* grows in dense clumps in fairly dry, open places, from 1'-3½' tall; generally with one to few large, yellow (white in one species), flower heads; basal leaves usually quite large. In the Common Mountain Mule Ears, *W. mollis*, (illustrated), the foliage is white woolly when young, turning to greenish when older. Stock and deer eat the flowers.

Indians used the roots as food, fermenting them on heated stones in the ground for one or two days. The flavor is sweet and agreeable. Roots were also used as a poultice for relief of pains and bruises. A decoction of leaves was used as a bath, producing profuse sweating. It should never be taken internally, as it is considered POISONOUS. *Wyethia* is listed in homeopathic medicines as used for pharyngitis (a throat irritation common among singers and speakers) and for hay fever.

Klamath Indians used the mashed roots as a poultice for swellings. Nevada Indians ground the resinous roots and soaked them in water to make a solution that was taken as an emetic (to induce vomiting). Often, for this purpose, they boiled the roots until the solution became quite concentrated. A combination remedy is to make a tea by boiling the chopped roots with the end twigs of the juniper (*Juniperus utahensis*), and take for colds and fevers. Habitat: Meadows; chaparral or brush; oak woodland; coastal coniferous forest; montane coniferous forest. Most states, and w. Canada.

NETTLES, *Urtica* species
(Nettle Family)

The six western species are all covered with stinging hairs, and have opposite, 3-7-nerved, toothed leaves; the flowers form clusters at the axils of the hairy or smooth leaves.

Pepys, in 1661, speaks of eating nettle porridge; also eaten in northern Persia. Scotch and Irish use the young leaves for greens. The French make seven different dishes from the nettle tops. Stems have an excellent fiber, used for fish lines and clothes.

Indians used branches to strike parts affected by pains, and a decoction of roots to bathe rheumatic pains in joints. Sometimes, pounded leaves rubbed on limbs produced a counter-irritant. Hot poultices of the mashed leaves were used for rheumatism. Habitat: Coastal coniferous forest; montane coniferous forest; meadows; streamside woodland. Most states.

PENSTEMON, *Penstemon* spp.
(Figwort Family)

(*P. gracilentus*, Slender Penstemon, illustrated.) There are numerous species, mostly herbs, but a few are shrubs; noted for long tube-like, showy flowers, red, blue, purple, yellow or white in color; opposite leaves; flowers irregular.

Spanish New Mexicans boil flowering tops and drink liquid for kidney trouble. Indians made a wash and a poultice for running sores; also steeped tops for colds. Red penstemons were boiled and the solution used as a wash for burns. It is said to stop pain and help new skin to grow. Most habitats. Most states, and w. Canada.

POISON HEMLOCK, *Conium maculatum*
(Carrot Family)

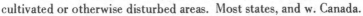

Herb, 1½'-10' tall, many-branched, with umbels of numerous, small, white flowers, and parsley-like leaves; grows in moist soil.

POISONOUS. Indians crush-ed seeds and mixed them with de-composed deer liver and used this to poison war arrows. Young spring leaves are poisonous to cattle. Habi-tat: Streamside woodland; meadows; cultivated or otherwise disturbed areas. Most states, and w. Canada.

POKEWEED, Pigeon Berry, Red-Ink Plant, *Phytolacca* spp.
(Pokeweed Family)

A large, coarse herb, 3'-4' high, with large, pointed leaves, pur-plish stem, thick fleshy root; greenish-white flowers in racemes; berries with crimson juice; seeds glossy black-purple.

Indians dried root and fruit, and used as purgative and emetic. Chinese dug root of one species in second and eighth months. They boiled leaves as pot herb. Young pokeweed shoots can be dug in the spring, boiled in two waters; in second water a bit of fat pork is added

and all is served as greens with vine-gar. The plant contains a bitter acidic poison, saponin, the root being most POISONOUS. From large roots, pokeweed shoots will re-new themselves again and again af-ter each cutting (cut at a foot or two high, before it turns purple), fur-nishing an excellent winter and early spring vegetable if kept away from frost. Medicinally the root was used for skin diseases, rheumatism and glandular swellings. It acts on the thyroid gland. The juice of the ber-ries was used for coloring frosting and candies. Habitat: Cultivated or otherwise disturbed areas. Calif.

PRAIRIE FLAX, *Linum lewisii*
(Flax Family)

Herb, 8"-36" high, many-branched, erect-growing and with woody rootstock; flowers blue in terminal clusters.

Indians used seeds in cooking, as they have a pleasant taste and are highly nutritious. Stems steeped for stomach disorders, and roots were steeped for eye medicine. Fiber was used as string. The whole plant was mashed and soaked in cold water to make an eye medicine. Poultices of the crushed fresh leaves were used to reduce swellings, especially goiter and for gall trouble. Early settlers made a poultice of the powdered seed, corn meal and boiling water, mixing this into a paste for infected wounds and mumps.

Pharmacopia says, "Reported useful in rheumatism, catarrhal infections, liver complaints and dropsy." Habitat: Grassland; meadows; oak woodland; montane coniferous forest. Most states, and w. Canada.

ST. JOHN'S WORT, **Klamath Weed,** *Hypericum* spp.
(St. John's Wort Family)

Herb 8"-32" high, sending out numerous stems from a woody rootstock; opposite leaves; flowers are yellow, five-petaled and in rather close clusters. It prefers poor, dry soil.

Parkinson (1640) wrote: "Was prepared as an ointment for external use, also as a decoction in wine to drink. A powder was made of the seeds and drunk in juice of knot grass to help all manner of spitting or vomiting of blood be it in any vein, broken inward by bruises or falls."

Indians ate the fresh leaves or dried the plant and made a flour that was used in the same way as acorn meal. It was also boiled and used for running sores. A yellow dye is made by boiling in alum water. *H. scouleri*, Scouler's St. John's Wort (illustrated) was boiled and water used for sores, etc. Habitat: Streamside woodland; meadows; cultivated or otherwise disturbed areas. Most states; and w. Canada.

SEGO LILY, *Calochortus nuttallii*
(Lily Family)

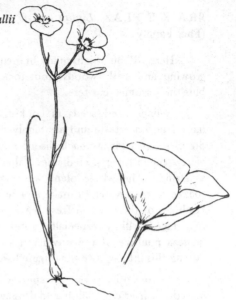

There were several species of *Calochortus* used by the Indians. All are told by the few, showy flowers (white, rose, purple, red, or yellow), each with petals marked with dark spots, blotches or lines.

Indians dug the bulbs when first flower buds appeared, roasted them in ashes after fire had died down, and also steamed them. Seeds were parched for pinole meal. Habitat: Grassland; oak woodland; montane coniferous forest; sagebrush scrub; pinyon-juniper woodland. Most states.

SHEPHERD'S PURSE, *Capsella bursa-pastoris*
(Mustard Family)

Herb, 3"-24" tall; stem single, with branching, deeply cut basal leaves that have a peppery flavor; tiny white flowers become triangular pods.

Used as a pot herb, it tastes like cabbage; also young leaves eaten raw. Indians roasted seeds and used as a nutritious meal.

An infusion of one ounce of leaves in 12 quarts of water is a remedy for bruises; taken internally it stops bleeding. Most habitats. Most states, and w. Canada.

SKUNKWEED, *Navarretia squarrosa* (Phlox Family) .

Herb, 2"-20" high, with white woolly leaves; about 1 " long, coarsely divided; flowers pale blue or purple in terminal heads; foliage has strong odor.

Indians gathered seeds in late summer, dried and stored them. To prepare them for eating, they would parch and pulverize the seeds and eat them dry.

Other species of *Navarretia* may have same odor and be used in same ways. White Navarretia, *N. leucocephala* (white flowers and with white or reddish-streaked stems), was boiled and decoction put on swellings. Habitat: Grassland; oak woodland; montane coniferous forest; coastal coniferous forest. Wash., Oreg., Calif., and w. Canada.

SMALL-FLOWERED NIGHTSHADE, *Solanum nodiflorum* (Nightshade Family)

Usually called Black Nightshade, because it is so much like the rarer weed, *S. nigrum.* Both have similar properties, but *nodiflorum* has 1'-2'-long straggling stems, while *nigrum* is more erect, 1'-3' high, and has dull instead of shining black berries. Both have white flowers.

Berries are POISONOUS, but boiling destroys the toxic properties in the ripe, black berries, and they were often made into pies. Although the old leaves are poisonous, it is said that young leaves and stems can be boiled as a pot herb. Indians used a decoction as an eyewash. Parkinson wrote: "The root boiled in wine and a little thereof held in the mouth eases the pain of toothache." Pliny wrote: "It is good to fasten loose teeth, and the juice of the root, mingled with honey, is good for weak eyes. Juice of the leaves and a little vinegar mixed together procures rest and sleep." Habitat: Grassland. Most states.

SQUAWROOT, Yampah, *Perideridia gairdneri* (Carrot Family)

Also called Caraway. A tall plant with single stem, 1'-3½' tall, with single umbels of white flowers, few, undivided leaves; fleshy roots single or in clusters; several bractlets surround flowers.

Parkinson, in 1640, writes: "Seeds good for colds or indigestions. A poultice made of powdered seeds is good for the eyes and will also take away black and blue spots. The herb and seed fried and put into a bag eases stomach pains."

The Indians gathered roots in the spring and washed them, trampled them to release the outer skin, then washed again and cooked as potatoes. Roots were ground and made into cakes also. Fremont liked it cooked with wild duck. Habitat: Meadows; streamside woodland. Most states, and w. Canada.

SWEET FENNEL, (miscalled "Anise"), *Foeniculum vulgare* (Carrot Family)

Herb, 2'-7' high, with very finely divided, grayish-light-green leaves, all with a sweet, anise smell; tiny yellow flowers in compound, flat umbels on long stems.

Parkinson, in 1640, writes: "Oil from seed sweetens breath, helps sleep, good for head and stomach consumption. Decoction with figs and licorice for coughs; boiled in wine, will help obstructions of liver; oil taken in broth helps dizziness. Plant, either green or dry, beaten and laid on eyes, will draw out bits and likewise take away hurt from (bites of) venomous creatures. Having infused bruised seed in wine 24 hours, then pressed and distilled, the residue in bottom will be like honey and can be kept for future use."

Curtin, in his Healing Herbs of the Rio Grande, says: "The cavaliers of 16th Century England believed that the seed, bound in a little bag or handkerchief and kept to the nose to smell, helps men from dreaming and starting in their sleep, and causes them to rest well." The Mission Fathers would sprinkle the floors with water in which the leaves were crushed to make the floors smell sweet. Indians used seeds for digestive troubles and gathered the young shoots to use as a pot herb. Tea from the roots was used for colds, and the leaves were chewed for a physic. Habitat: Grassland; cultivated or disturbed areas. California.

TURKEY-MULLEIN, Dove Weed, *Eremocarpus setigerus* (Spurge Family)

A low-growing bush, 5"-8" high, with heavy-scented gray foliage, in dry, open areas from Washington to Lower California. Greenish flowers; dark gray, shining seeds; stinging hairs.

As the leaves contain a narcotic poison, Indians used the foliage to stupefy fish and poison their arrow points. A poultice relieved internal chest pains and a decoction of leaves in warm water helped asthma and fevers. Pharmacopia says used to expel gas. Habitat: Sagebrush scrub; grassland; oak woodland; cultivated or otherwise disturbed areas. Washington, Oregon, and California.

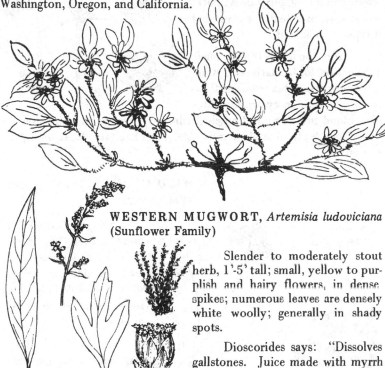

WESTERN MUGWORT, *Artemisia ludoviciana* (Sunflower Family)

Slender to moderately stout herb, 1'-5' tall; small, yellow to purplish and hairy flowers, in dense spikes; numerous leaves are densely white woolly; generally in shady spots.

Dioscorides says: "Dissolves gallstones. Juice made with myrrh works with same effect as do the roots; also being made up with axungia (hog or goose grease) into an ointment, takes away wens and hard knots.

"Three drams of the powder of dried leaves taken in wine is a speedy and best cure for sciatica (a painful affliction of the hip)." Pliny says: "If a traveler bind some of the herb about him, he will feel no weariness on his journey."

Indians used it medicinally by making a decoction of the leaves for colds, colic, bronchitis, rheumatism and fever. A poultice was made for wounds, and the juice was used for poison oak. A leaf inserted in one nostril was supposed to cure headache.

WILD BUCKWHEAT, *Eriogonum* spp.
(Buckwheat Family)

(*E. baileyi* illustrated, right). There are about 150 species in a growth range from sea level to high mountains. All varieties seem to like more or less dry and rocky slopes and ridges. Most buckwheats grow on medium tall stems, loosely branched, with white to pinkish flowers in clusters or heads.

Because of its long blooming season and fine-quality honey, buckwheat is an excellent bee plant, but it is poor stock feed.

From the leaves Indians made a decoction for headache and stomach pains; also, a tea from the flowers was used as an eyewash and for high blood pressure and bronchial ailments. The stems and leaves are boiled for a tea to treat bladder trouble. Most habitats. Most states, and w. Canada.

WILD CLOVER, *Trifolium* spp.
(Pea Family)

(*T. gracilentum*, Pinpoint Clover, illustrated.) Small herbs with typical 3 leaflets and flowers yellow, white or purple in heads or short spikes; stamens two-grouped.

In Scotland, bread was made from the White Clover (*T. repens*), and the pioneers made clover tea, brewing dried flower heads. Indians ate it raw or steamed and the steamed plant was dried for winter use.

White clover was not cooked, but eaten raw, both flowers and leaves, but if too much was consumed, it would produce bloat, and, to counteract this effect, the leaves were dipped in salted water. Most habitats. Most states, and w. Canada.

WILD ONIONS, *Allium* spp.
(Lily Family)

The long, slender leaves and the onion-smelling foliage are typical. It was mainly the larger species with large bulbs that Indians used.

Aztecs chewed the bulbs to relieve flatulency and as food. California Indians ate the bulbs raw and cooked them also over hot ashes. The whole plant was used as an insect repellant by rubbing on the body. It is reputed to be useful as a diuretic (increasing the flow of urine) in kidney disorders.

Flowers are rose, reddish-purple and white in color; leaves 2"-4" or more high. Habitat: Ponds, streams, etc.; streamside woodland; meadows; marshlands. Most states and w. Canada.

YERBA MANSA, *Anemopsis californica*
(Lizard's Tail Family)

Plant 6"-24" tall, with a creeping rootstock, and white flowers in dense spikes surrounded by petal-like bracts; the heart-shaped leaves are mostly basal. The plant has a pungent, spicy odor, and the aromatic root was chewed raw.

Tea made of the leaves was used for purifying blood; a poultice for cuts and bruises; and bruised leaves reduced swellings, dysentery, asthma. The tea was also used for colds and to help movement of urine in kidney ailments. An infusion of the rootstocks was used for various skin troubles. The leaves boiled in a quantity of water were used as a bath for muscular pains and for sore feet. Dried roots, roasted and browned, were made into a decoction used for colds and for stomach ache. Habitat: Montane coniferous forest; meadows; streamside woodland. California, Ariz., Nev., N.M., and Texas.

INDEX OF COMMON NAMES

INDEX OF GENERA